I'M OVER 50 AND I WANT TO LEARN TO

Creating email, text messages, and Facetime with your iPad

Based upon the Apple iPad Guide

by

Iburia V. Hall-Haynes, Ph.D.

* * * * *

Copyright 2014

ISBN: 978-1496119568

Thank you for purchasing this resource manual. Please do not reprint it without permission. Consider making additional purchases for friends and family members. Additional copies can be purchased for workshops, senior citizen homes, and as gifts for those who would like a little more assistance. Thank you for your interest and support.

This is your personal workbook. You will be able to make notes and complete activities as you become more familiar with your iPad.

Dedication

This book is dedicated to my mother, Luvenia W. Hall, for instilling in me a "never give up" spirit; my husband, Edwin L. Haynes, I, for being with me through thick and thin; my son, Edwin L. Haynes, II, for making me laugh and encouraging me as "he is having fun"; and my daughter Edneka L. Haynes, for being such a joy and providing hope for our future. Because of them, I am certain that this book is the first of many.

Table of Contents

Dedication ii

Preface v

Overview of Teminology vi

What are Applications (Apps)? 2

The iPad 4

Safari 6

What are some of the basic parts of the iPad? 7

Activity #1 9

    Locating iPad parts and defining icons/Apps 9

What are the functions of iPad icons/Apps? 10

Activity #2 11

    Review of the functions of iPad icons/Apps 11

Apps Review 12

What is the function of iPad settings? 12

Activity #3 14

    Review the Settings options 14

Settings OptionsApplications (Apps) 14

    Steps for accessing Apps 15

    Apps on iPad 16

How do I enter text using the keyboard? 16

Activity #4 18

    Identify the basic parts of the iPad, Apps and Enter Text on Keyboard 18

How do I enter data using the keyboard? 20

Activity #5 21

Practice entering data/text using the keyboard 21

How do I create contacts? 23

Activity #6 27

Practice creating contacts 27

How do I create and send text messages? 28

Activity #7 29

Create a text message 29

How do I send and receive email? 30

Activity #8 33

Create an email 33

FaceTime 34

How do I use FaceTime? 35

Activity #9 36

Practice making FaceTime calls 36

Photos and Videos 37

How do I send photos and videos? 37

Activity #10 38

Practice taking photos and videos 38

What is Siri? 39

How do I type and enter text with keyboard and Siri? 41

Activity #11 42

Practice using Siri 42

Icon Summary 43

Summary 46

Preface

This resource manual is designed to simplify the use of the iPad for seniors and anyone who wants to learn more about this device. It is described in everyday terms and will reduce some of the frustrations associated with operating this kind of tool. Opportunities are given to explore the various applications through related activities. Seniors are warned not to make purchases without all of the details. *(Before making purchases, they should understand exactly what they are buying).* This manual focuses on the iPad primarily; however, the iPad and iPhone operate essentially the same way. The activities will help to build confidence and familiarize readers with the functions of the iPad. We begin by defining some of the basic terms.

Overview of Teminology

It is important that you begin by familiarizing yourself with some of the basic terminology that is associated with using the iPad. When you become familiar, you will notice that your comfort level with this technology will improve.

App -- App is short for applications. Applications are the programs on the iPad such as iTunes, Safari, Google, and etc.

Contacts -- our friends, family members and businesses that we have dealings with. We create contacts because that is the way we will send text messages, email, make FaceTime calls and phone our friends and family.

FaceTime camera -- an application on the iPad that allows you to see the face of the person you are talking to on the phone or iPad after a call is made.

iPad -- a small, but powerful computer that allows users to access the internet, send and receive mail, and participate in FaceTime conversations.

Icons -- pictures or buttons found on the face of the iPad.

Multi-touch display -- the iPad allows the user to drag, tap, and rearrange the icons *(similar to desktop on computers)*.

Scrolling -- to cause displayed text or graphics to move up, down, or across the screen *(scroll from left to right or up and down)*.

Status bar -- the information above the icons (pictures) on the iPad that shows the network status, time and battery information.

When you select each App, pay close attention to the options available. For example, when you click on the **Message** icon you will be able to: 1). select a name from your contacts list; 2). edit your contacts; 3). add to your contacts; 4) search for names; and 5). create a message. It is important to pay particular attention to all of the options available when you select the various Apps. A good question to ask is, What can I do with this App?

iPad Overview

Picture of Slider bar

I am pleased that you have decided to learn to use your iPad. One of the first things that you need to do is become comfortable with all of the parts of the iPad.

At first, the slider bar may seem difficult to slide, but lightly drag the arrow on the iPad from left to right with the tip of your index finger. This takes you to the main menu options or applications/apps screen. It says "slide to unlock".

The slider bar unlocks the screen. Make sure you practice powering down (turning off) the iPad and then turning it back on again. You will find as you progress that the more familiar you become, the better. We will focus on five major functions of the iPad: *creating contacts*, *creating texts*, *creating messages*, using Siri, and *creating FaceTime calls*.

Enjoy the journey!

What are Applications (Apps)?

Applications/Apps found on iPad

Definitions

The 20 Apps are described from left to right in order. The picture or icons respresent the Apps or applications on the iPad. *See icons/pictures above.*

1. **Message**—used to create text messages.
2. **FaceTime**—used to see the person you are talking to face-to-face. Both parties must have Wi-Fi connections.
3. **Photos**—used to store pictures—much like a regular camera.
4. **Camera**—used to take pictures. Click and focus on target item.

5. **Maps**—used to obtain directions both written and orally as you drive or walk.

6. **Clock**—used to set the time and alarms.

7. **Photo Booth**—used to alter pictures with creative looks.

8. **Calendar**—used to help you keep tract of the date.

9. **Contacts**—names and email addresses used for texting and FaceTime.

10. **Notes**—permits you to type notes to yourself.

11. **Reminders**—permits you to type specific reminders to yourself.

12. **Newsstand**—allows you to purchase newspapers and magazines.

13. **iTunes**—permits you to buy music, albums and online games.

14. **App Store**—permits you to buy Apple Apps.

15. **Game Center**—permits you to purchase games or download free games.

16. **Settings**—the heart of the iPad. This is the area where you set the sound, keyboard, Wi-Fi, notifications, privacy settings and etc.

17. **Safari**—lets you get on the internet to type desired addresses and surf the Web.

18. **Mail**—lets you create email.

19. **Video**—lets you create videos.

20. **Music**—lets you download music thru iTunes.

To rearrange the icons on you iPad, press and hold the **Apps picture**. The pictures begin to "shimmy" or "wiggle". At this point, drag the pictures or icons to where you would like, and then press the **Home Button**. *Wallah!*

The iPad

Front   **Back**

Front and Back view of the iPad

The volume up and down button is found on the right side. *Remember to press firmly.*

How do I turn the iPad on and off?

The iPad is turned on and off by pressing the On/Off button on the top right corner of the computer. *It's not easy to see.*

You should press the button hard and hold it down to turn it on and off.

When it comes on you will see a Slider bar at the button. The Slider bar may only be set to appear a few seconds. Don't worry, just press the On/Off button again and slide the slider bar arrow to the right. You may have to do this more than once. *Again, don't worry just do it again LOL.*

Oh yes, to turn the iPad off, press and hold the On/Off button again. *It may feel like it's taking forever, hang in there! It is slow sometimes.*

Remember, hold down the On/Off button firmly to turn the iPad on, and unlock the slider bar at the bottom of the computer. To turn the iPad off, hold down the On/Off button firmly.

Safari

Let's learn how to use Safari. This web browser is generally the default browser on your iPad. To begin working with Safari, go to settings and select Safari under the settings tab. Then, select the options under the Safari tab that you would like.

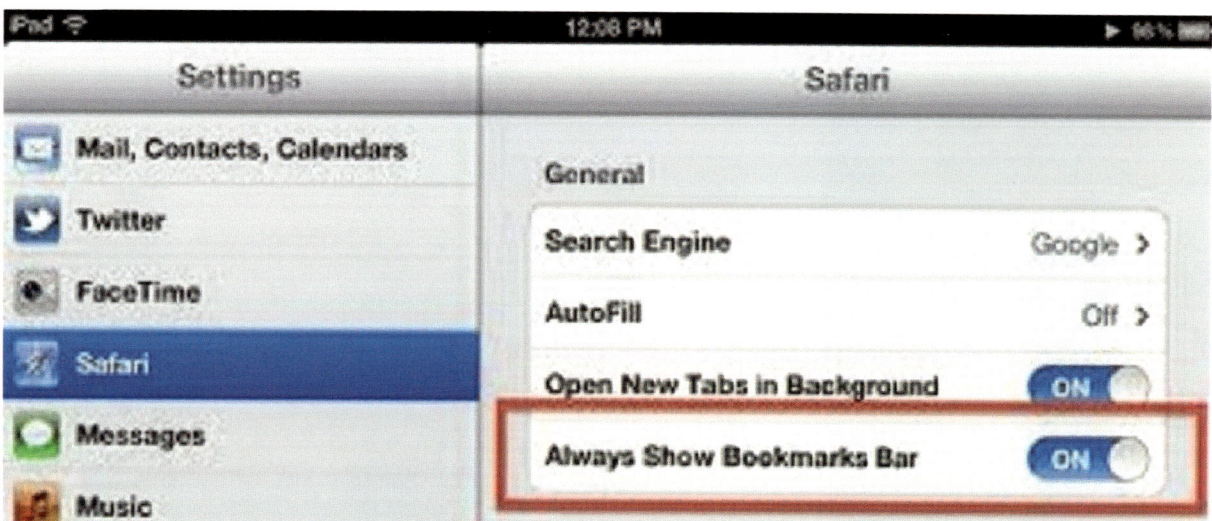

Safari and similar browers are important because they allow you to access email accounts and websites. Remember the goal of this manual is to help you learn to *create contacts*, *create text messages*, use *Siri*, and make *FaceTime calls*. You will find that looking up information with this web browser is fascinating. The addresses that you look up will remain in the history (sites visited) until you delete them. This makes it very easy to return to visited sites.

You look up information by using the touchscreen on your iPad. Zooming in is one of the features of your iPad. When you type the information or ask Siri to locate a site for you, you can zoom in and out and scroll by touching the screen in a specific way or pinching the screen.

You can open up to nine web pages at a time. That helps when you want to view several sites and go back and forth. By clicking on the tab or the site you can go from one to another.

While you are conducting research, looking up medical information, or visiting your friends' websites, you may listen to music, write that novel you have always wanted to write, modify settings, or simply work on or multi-task while using your iPad.

Practice double-tapping in a blank area of your screen. A larger screen size appears. Double tap the menu once again and the screen will zoom out to the standard view again. You can also pinch the screen with the thumb and index finger. Set them on the spot that you want to enlarge and slowly spread your thumb and index finger away from each other on the screen.

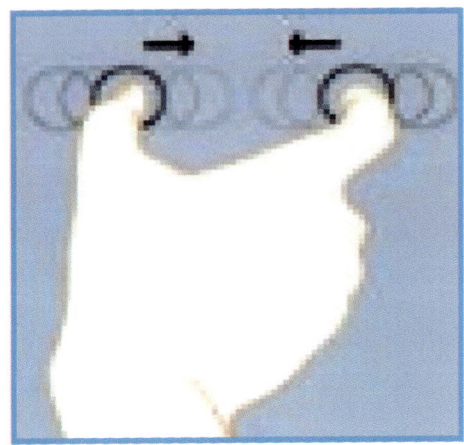

What are some of the basic parts of the iPad?

    The picture above illustrates the various icons/Apps. There are eleven (11) activities in this resource manual that coincide with the topics. They are designed to help you build the confidence that is necessary to master the use of your iPad. We start by becoming familiar with all of the icons (pictures). You will find that each picture actually represents the actions you will take.

Activity #1

Locating iPad parts and defining icons/Apps

Locate the On/Off button on your iPad.

1. Where is it located?
_____

2. How long should you hold it down?
_____

Practice holding it down.

3. What happens when you hold it down?
_____

4. Which direction should you slide the slider bar?
_____

5. How do you turn your iPad off?
_____

Practice turning it on and off.

Note: To lock your screen and avoid redials or opening Apps, press the On/Off button. Hold it. To turn off completely, hold longer (LOL). The Apple icon appears when you turn in on. Make sure you unlock the screen before it goes into sleep mode. If it does, just press the Home button at the bottom.

Based upon the previous definitions, how would you define:
iTunes App_____
Safari   _____
Calendar   _____

9

What are the functions of iPad icons/Apps?

Picture of icons/Apps

    The icons or pictures are very important. They represent the functions of the applications that are a part of the iPad.

    There are 20 icons in the picture above. To open the Apps (Applications), tap on them. Believe it or not, when they are opened, if you complete the guided prompts, you will be able to utilize the applications. *Trust Yourself.*

Activity #2

Review of the functions of iPad icons/Apps

Review each App and their functions again.

1. Which App would you use to create a text message?
_____

2. Which App would you use to set the alarm clock?
_____

3. Which App would you use to create an email?
_____

4. Which App would you use to create FaceTime?
_____

5. Which App would you use to go to the Internet?
_____

6. Which App would you use to take a picture?
_____

How many Apps can you define without looking at the definitions? **List them below.**

1. _____
2. _____
3. _____
4. _____

5. _____
6. _____
7. _____
8. _____
9. _____
10. _____
11. _____
12. _____
13. _____

Apps Review

What happens after I turn the iPad on?

To operate your iPad efficiently, you need to set up an email account and an Apple ID. Free mail accounts can be set up through *AOL*, *Yahoo*, *Hotmail*, *Google*, and etc.

Google, *Safari* and *Internet Explorer* are three of the most popular browsers. Browsers are used to access the Internet or go online. After going online, if you want to go to a specific site, type the Universal Resource Locator (URL) on the address line. (Example: http://www.google.com).

What is the function of iPad settings?

An internet connection is needed to access the internet (broadband is recommended). Some iPads have mobile Wi-Fi and do not require additional connections. The Apple ID is used with *iCloud, the App Store* and *iTunes Store,* and online purchases.

Your iPad comes installed with the operating system that you need. iTunes purchases (movies, CDs, DVDS, etc.) can be made at:

http:// www.itunes.com/download

The settings icon will allow you to:

*Connect to a Wi-Fi network

*Sign in with or create a free Apple ID account

*Set up iCloud if you didn't earlier

*Select those features you would like to turn on

After these settings are completed initially, they do not need to be reset. In most cases, they have been set up for you earlier by your children or friends. Becoming familiar with the iPad is essential. Take your time and get comfortable. **Don't panic**, it may take a few weeks to become entirely comfortable. At least that's what happened to me (LOL). Make sure you have created an email account first and added it to your iPad.

Activity #3

Review the Settings options

To review the options in the Settings:

1. Tap the settings icon

2. Review the various options

3. Look at settings column

Lots of options! You will become more comfortable with these settings as you use them more.

Don't change anything yet. Just make sure that you are aware of the kinds of things you can do with this Application.

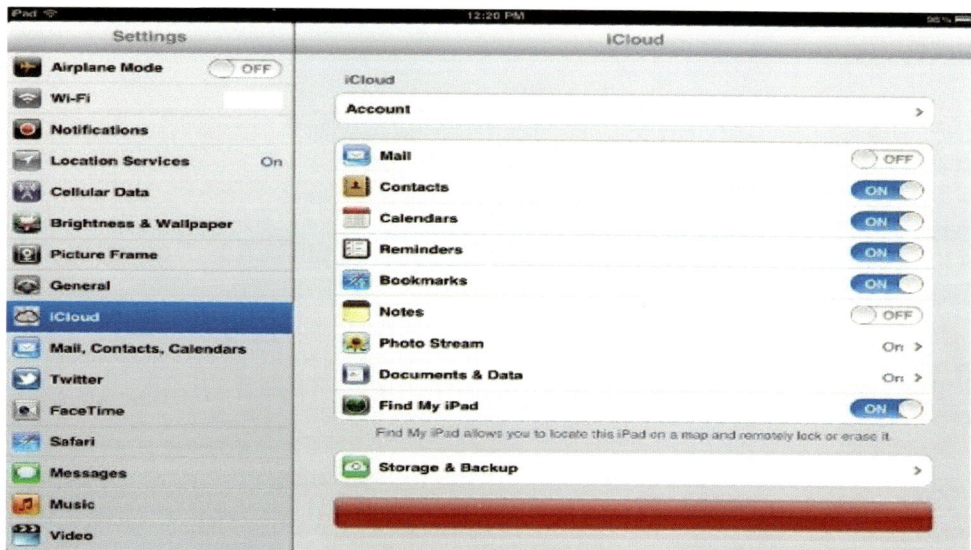

Settings Options

Applications (Apps)

Apps are the programs that are on your iPad screen. You select programs on your iPad by using your fingers to tap, double-tap, swipe, and pinch objects on the touchscreen.

Steps for accessing Apps

To go to the Home screen, press the Home button.

When you go to an App or location you do not want to go to, go back Home by pressing the Home button.

To open the Message App, Tap it.

Home icon / Button

Home icon/Button

Apps on iPad

To return to the Home screen, press the Home button again. *(If you end up some place you're not sure of, press the Home button again).*

Tap an App to use it again. Drag the screen to the left to see more applications. As you download more Apps, you will need to drag to the left to see them.

As you type, each letter appears above your thumb or finger. If you touch the wrong key, you can slide your finger to the correct key. The letter isn't entered until you release your finger from the key.

How do I enter text using the keyboard?

To type in all capital letters.

Tap the Shift key before tapping a letter. *Or touch and hold the Shift key, then type the letter.*

Turn on caps lock.

Double-tap the Shift key to turn caps lock off, tap the Shift key.

To enter numbers, punctuation, or symbols.

Tap the Number key. *To see additional punctuation and symbols, tap the Symbol key.*

Editing text

If you need to edit text, position the insertion point (|) where you need it. You can select, cut, copy, and paste text. In some Apps, you can also cut, copy, and paste photos and videos. Position the insertion point (|), touch and hold to bring up the magnifying glass, then drag to position the insertion point.

Select text

Tap the insertion point to display the selection buttons.

Tap, **Select** to select the word, or tap **Select All** to select all text.

Activity #4

Identify the basic parts of the iPad, Apps and Enter Text on Keyboard

1. Where is the Home Button?
   _____

2. What is its purpose?
   _____

3. Find the Text Messaging icon, what is its purpose?
   _____

4. If you want to go to the Internet, which icon will you tap?
   _____

5. Which icon allows you to take a picture?
   _____

Take a moment to practice tapping, double tapping, and touching the screen to open the App

6. What is the Home button/icon used for?
   _____

7. If you somehow end up on a screen that you don't want to be on, what button do you press to go back to the icon choices?
   _____

Apps on iPad

Portrait and landscape orientation

You can view many iPad Apps in either portrait (looks like a picture) or landscape (a picture rotated 90 degrees) orientation.

If you rotate iPad and the screen rotates, it will adjust to fit the new orientation.

How do I enter data using the keyboard?

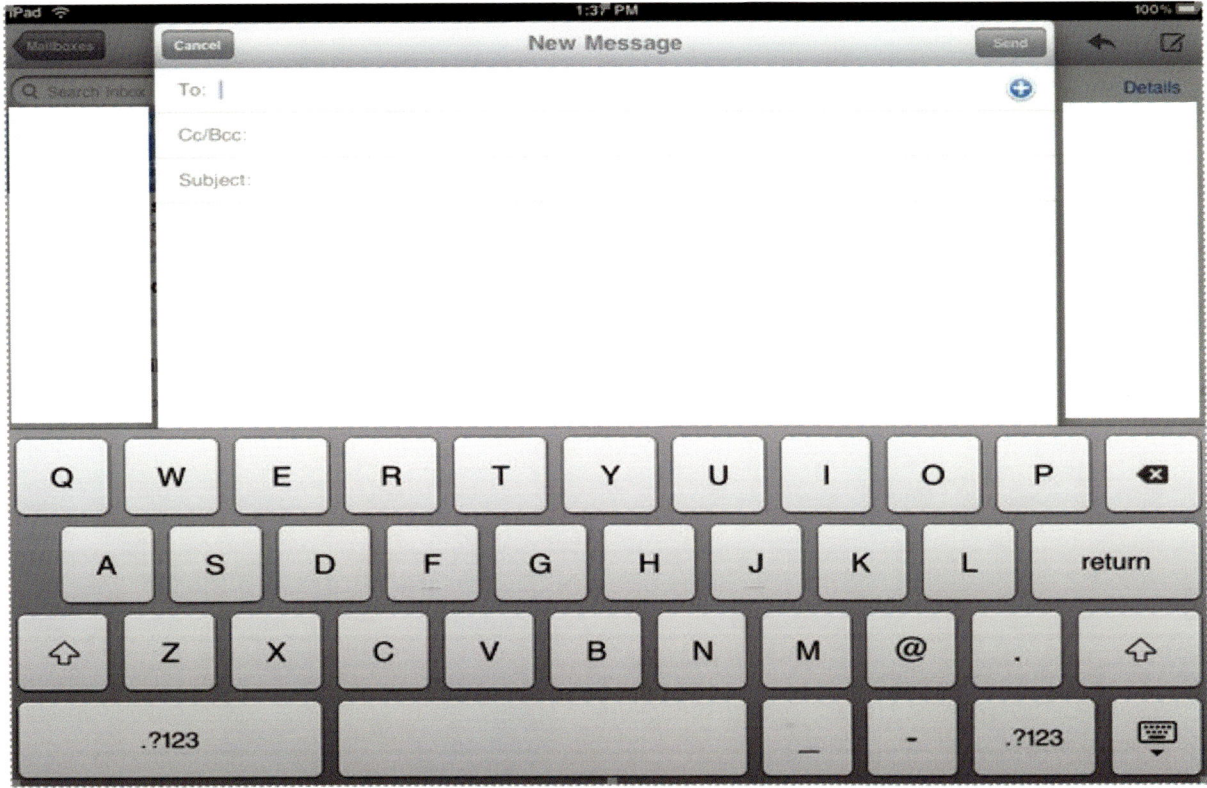

Typing on the keyboard lets you enter text. Use the onscreen keyboard to enter text, such as contact information, mail, and web addresses. Some applications may correct misspellings, predict what you're typing, and even add words to your database dictionary as you use it.

To enter text, tap a text field to bring up the keyboard, then tap keys on the keyboard.

A text field is the white space after **To, Subject or Message** as shown in the picture above.

Activity #5

Practice entering data/text using the keyboard

1. Type your name in the text field on your iPad.

___

2. Type a message to someone you have not spoken to for some time.

___

3. How do you make the keyboard appear?

___.

How do I create contacts?

Saved phone numbers, emails and contact information make up your contacts.

Contacts are created by completing the following steps:

1. Touch the  picture

2. Set your **My Info** card

3. Go to Settings

4. Tap Mail

5. Tap Contacts

6. Tap **My Info** add and your information, or

7. Select the contact card with your name and information

The **My Info** card is used by **Siri** and other applications.

Use the related person's field to define relationships you want **Siri** to know about, so you can say things like "call my daughter."

Search contacts

1. Tap the search field at the top of the contact list and enter your search

2. You can also search your contacts from the Home screen.

3. Share a contact

4. Tap a contact, then tap Share Contact

You can search the contact info by email or message.

Add a contact

1. Tap

2. Enter contact information

3. Add a contact to your Favorites list

4. Choose a contact

5. Scroll down

6. Tap the Add to Favorites button

Delete a contact

1. Choose a contact

2. Tap Edit

3. Scroll down

4. Tap Delete Contact

Edit a contact

1. Choose a contact

2. Tap Edit

To add a new field

1. Tap

2. Choose or enter a label for the field

3. Change a field label

4. Tap the label and choose a different one

To add a custom field

   Tap Add Custom Label

Change the ringtone or text tone for the contact

1. Tap the ringtone or text tone field

2. Choose a new sound

To change the default tone for contacts, go to Settings and Sounds.

1. Assign a photo to the contact

2. Tap Add Photo

You can take a photo with the camera or use an existing photo.

Your Notes…..

Activity #6

Practice creating contacts

Create 5 Contacts on your iPad by following the steps previously outlined.

You can do it!

List your strategies for creating contacts…

How do I create and send text messages?

To create messages for friends, family members, and any contacts that you may have, follow the steps below:

1. Touch the ⬜ message icon

2. Tap this icon ⬜

   This icon lets you start a new message

3. Tap this icon ⊕

   This icon lets you see your contact list

4. Select the name of the person you would like to contact

   You can search for a name by typing a name or phone number.

If you do not see a list of names, type the phone number or email address of the person in the message section. **Click Send.**

You can do it!

As you can see, there are only a few steps in sending and receiving text messages. The text sends an abbreviated message to the iPad or cell phone.

You're going to love sending texts! Oh, by the way, clicking in the subject field will make the keyboard appear.

When you **receive a text message**, you will hear a sound. Touch your message ⬜ icon to retrieve it.

28

Activity #7

Create a text message

Create a Text Message on your iPad by following the steps on the previous page.

Good Luck!

The contact numbers will appear in the white space above. The actual message that you type will appear in the gray space.

When you see this symbol it means you can create a message.

29

How do I send and receive email?

You can send and receive email to and from friends, family members and any contacts that you may have. You can read and compose mail. Follow the steps below.

Sending mail

To compose a message…

1. Tap ▱ (the write icon -- this symbol/icon means to compose or write)
2. Type the names of intended recipients in the **To** field.
3. Type the names of those you wish to **Cc/Bcc** in that field.
4. Type the name of the **Subject** of your email.
5. Type your **message**.
6. Click **Send** after you have completed the message.

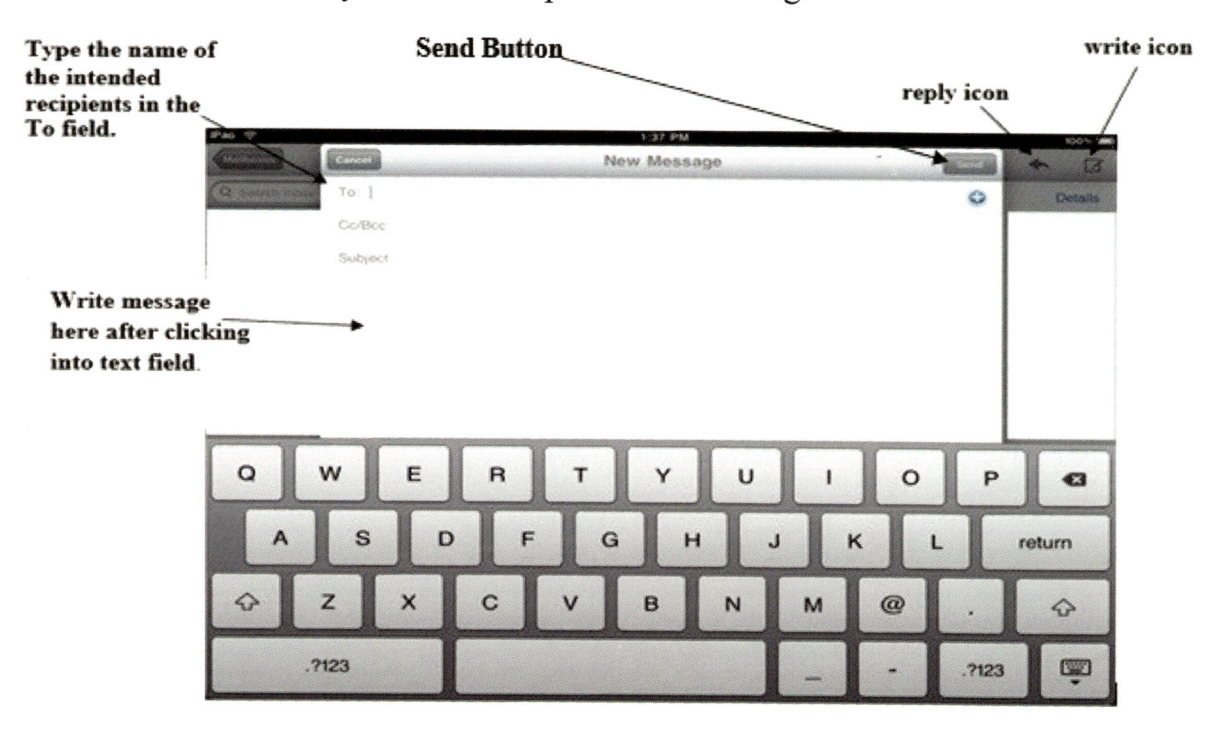

Type the name of the intended recipients in the To field.

Send Button

reply icon

write icon

Write message here after clicking into text field.

*In the **Cc/Bcc** field enter the name or names of the persons you would like to Cc (carbon copy) or Bcc (blind carbon copy) someone without anyone knowing that this person was carbon copied.*

To save a draft of a message

- Tap Cancel
- Tap Save Draft
- Touch and hold to see your saved drafts.

To reply to a message

- Tap ↰ then tap (this icon allows you to reply to the message).
- *To include the attachments, forward the message instead of replying.*

To forward a message

- Open a message and tap ↰ , then tap Forward.
- This also forwards the message's attachments.

To receive email

1. Click on the ✉ email icon.

When you click on the icon, the screen below appears. Mail boxes appear with the number of unread messages.

2. Click on this icon to compose or write a message.

The Search inbox appears below the mailboxes.

To reply to a message or email

See previous section on sending email

- To reply to a message or respond to someone who sent you a message, click on this button ↰ on the status bar of an incoming message. To include attachments, forward the message instead of replying.

31

To forward a message click on this ![icon]. You will be given several options. You can use this icon to:

- **reply** to the person who sent you the email
- **reply all** to a group of people who were on an email sent to you
- **forward** to a new person
- **print** to a network or local (connected) printer – printers will need to be added.

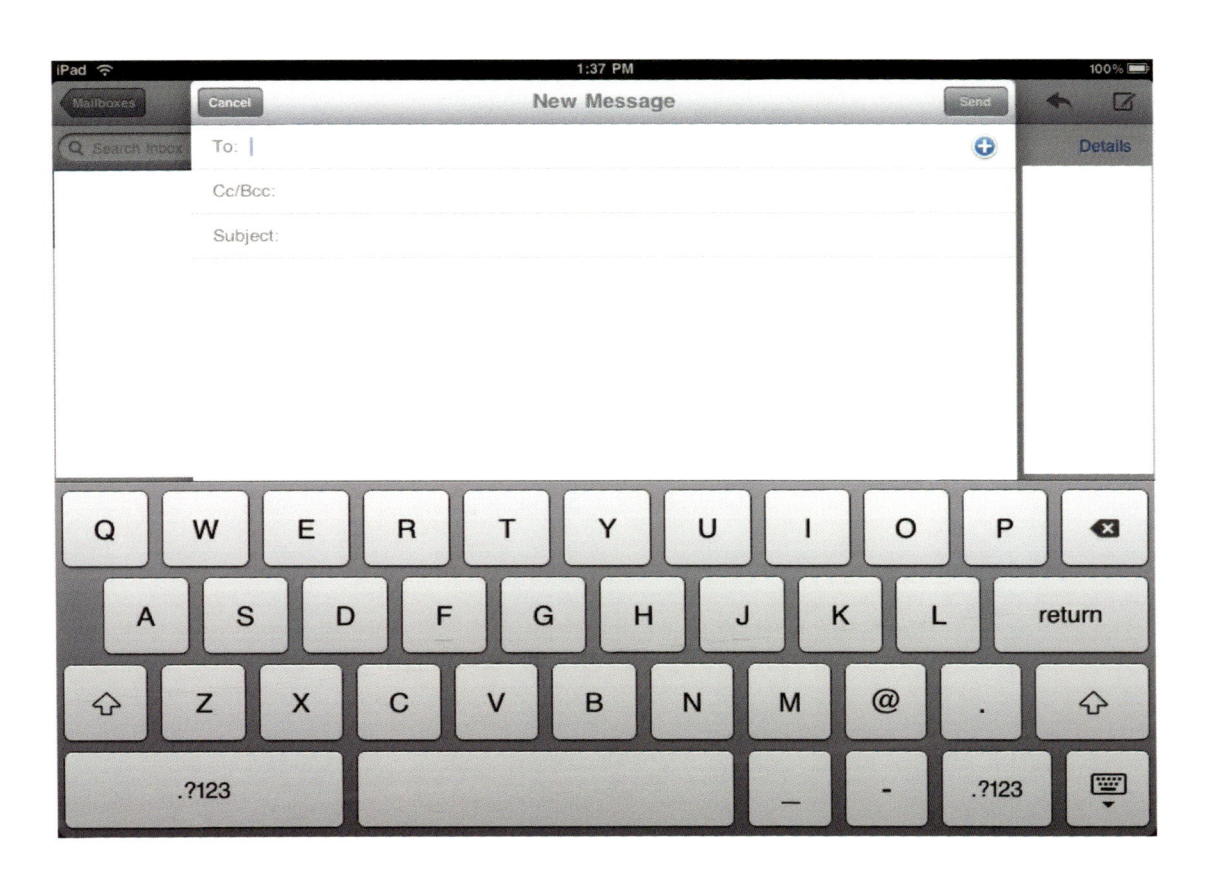

Activity #8

Create an email

Create an email on your iPad by following the steps on the previous pages.

Awesome! Review the status bar on top of the email picture. Notice that you can:

1. Save the messages to a folder

2. Delete them

3. Click the ⬅ that allows you to forward, reply, print, or write ✎ another email

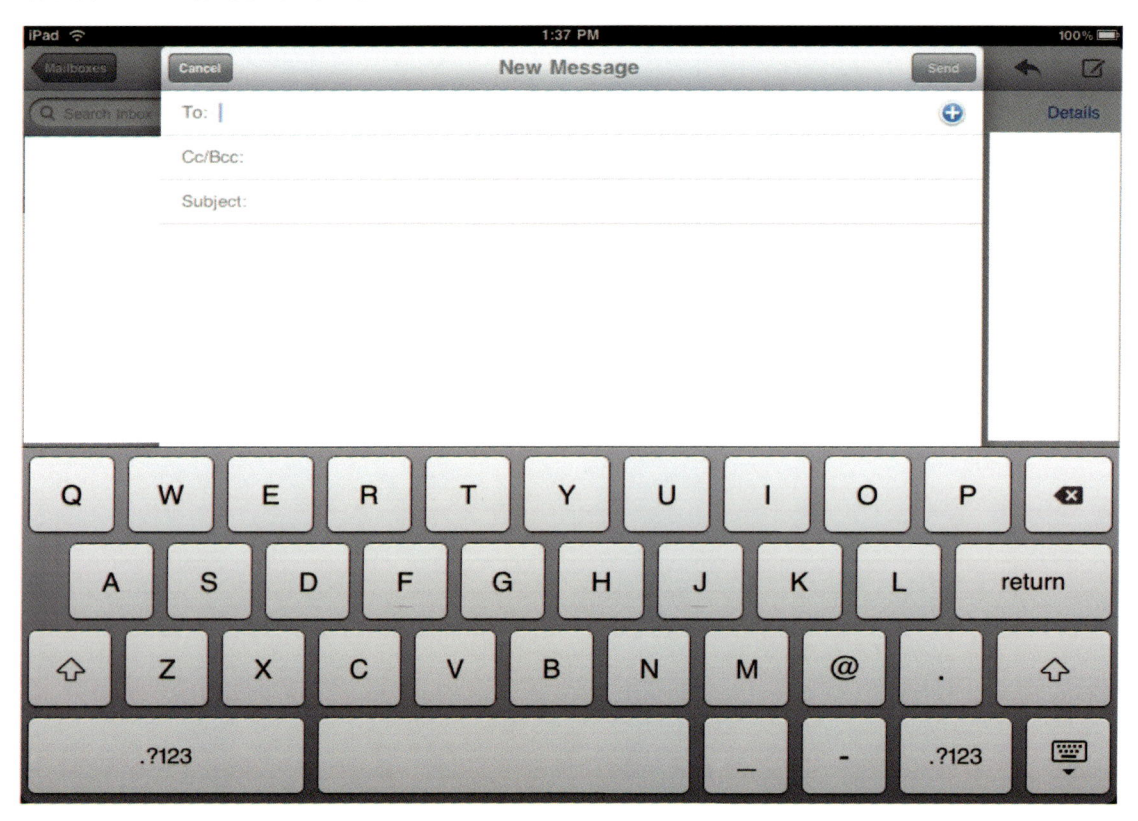

FaceTime

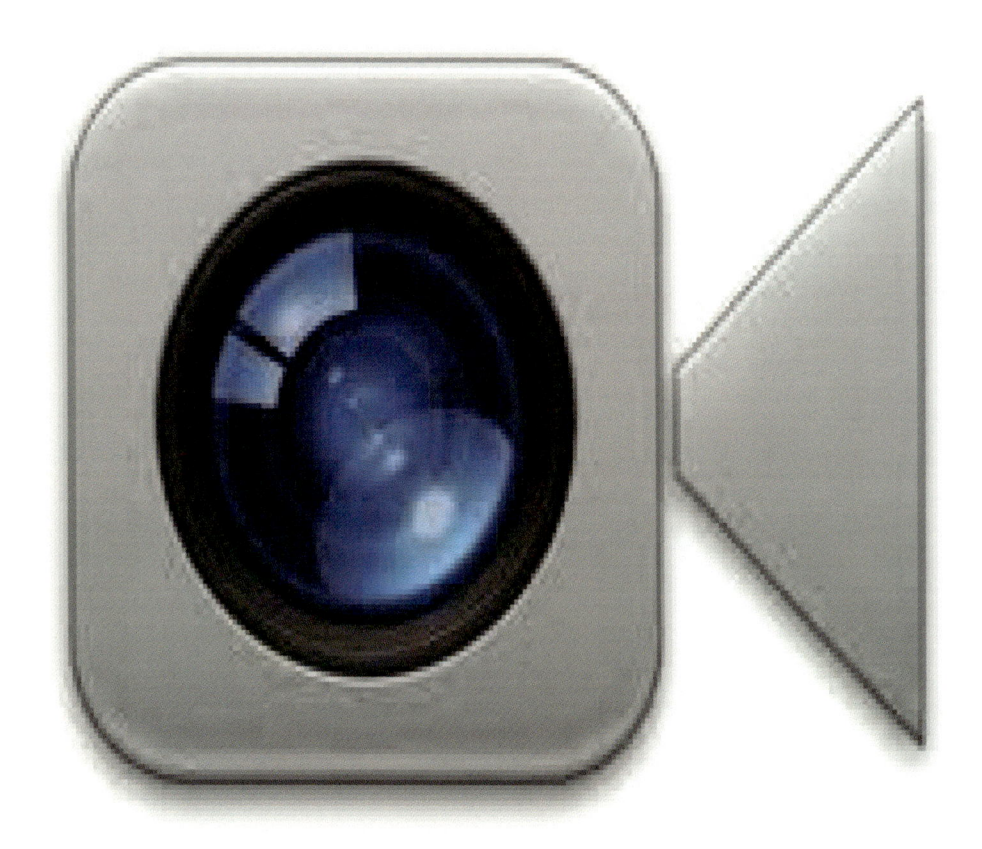

How do I use FaceTime?

You can make video or FaceTime calls to devices that support this kind of technology. The FaceTime camera lets you see the person you are communicating with.

FaceTime is not available on all computers or devices. To use FaceTime, you need an Apple ID and a WI-FI connection to the Internet. *Usually setup prior to actual use.*

1. Click on FaceTime icon

2. Tap Contacts

3. Choose a name

4. Tap the phone number or email address of the person you want to contact

You can also make a FaceTime call from the Contacts application.

Use a recent call

1. Tap recent

2. Choose the name and or number

To add a contact

1. Tap contacts

2. Tap

3. Enter the person's name and the email address or phone number

To set options for FaceTime

1. Go to settings

2. Go to FaceTime

5. Specify a phone number, Apple ID or email address to use FaceTime

Activity #9

Practice making FaceTime calls

Complete the activity below by reviewing the previous page.

Make a FaceTime call on your iPad by following the steps on the previous page.

Good Luck!

Who will you FaceTime first? Remember the person you FaceTime must have a FaceTime compatible iPad or phone.

Photos and Videos

How do I send photos and videos?

Review the steps below to send a photo or produce a video.

To copy a photo or video

1. Touch and hold the attachment/photo

2. Tap Copy

To save contact information you receive

1. Tap the contact bubble

2. Tap Create New Contact or Add to Existing Contacts

To add someone to your contacts from the Messages list

1. Tap the phone number or email address

2. Tap Add to Contacts *(Review Section on Contacts)*

Activity #10

Practice taking photos and videos

Review the previous steps to send a photo or produce a video.

1. Take a Photo and Video

2. Take a Photo and Video on your iPad by following those steps.

You can also use the iPad camera to take selfies or pictures you take of yourself.

Take a moment to review the options available for taking pictures.

What is Siri?

Siri is the feature on the iPad that lets you speak instructions and commands.

Siri is like a personal assistant. When you press the icon, **Siri** understands you when you talk.

You can tell **Siri,** for example, to:

    1. Call the Pizza Store

    2. Set the alarm for 10:30 p.m.

    3. Call Ed at 6:30 in the morning.

Siri lets you:

    1. Write and send a message

    2. Schedule a meeting

    3. Place a FaceTime call

    4. Get directions

    5. Set a reminder

Just speak naturally when you are talking to Siri, you can ask her to, for example...

1. FaceTime Barbara

2. Set the timer for 60 minutes while you cook dumplings

3. Get directions

4. Post to Facebook

5. Tweet

How do I type and enter text with keyboard and Siri?

You can manually enter text with the keyboard. Use the onscreen keyboard to enter text, such as contact information, mail, and web addresses. Now go to contacts. *See contacts sections.*

Tap in a text field to bring up the keyboard, then tap keys on the keyboard. (**Siri** is the microphone icon found on the bottom of the keyboard).

Text Field |_____(It is the search field also).

Keyboard Dictation & Siri

On an iPad that supports it, you can dictate text instead of typing. To use dictation, press the home key twice to bring up **Siri** or hold until **Siri** comes up. **Siri** must be turned on and iPad must be connected to the Internet. You can include punctuation and give commands to format your text.

1. Go to Settings
2. Go to **Siri**
3. Turn on **Siri**
4. Onscreen dictation
5. Tap on the keyboard
6. Tell **Siri** what you want
7. Finish by tapping

Activity #11

Practice using Siri

Use **Siri** to call someone or set up FaceTime on your iPad by following the steps on the previous page. *The best to you!*

1. Where is **Siri** located?
   _____

2. What does **Siri** do?
   _____

3. Press the dictation icon (**Siri**) and tell her to call one of your friends. Your friend's name must be in your Contacts.

4. Tap the **Siri** icon.

Get directions to your favorite restaurant. Write them here.

_____
_____
_____
_____

5. Tell **Siri** to set the alarm clock for 30 minutes.

Icon Summary

The next few pages summarize additional Apps on your iPad and iPhone.

Photo App

Your photos are in the Photo App

Click on it and you will see all of the pictures you have taken.

Maps

The Maps icon allows you to put an address in so that you can receive directions to a specific location.

Clock

The clock icon allows you to select from the following options:

1. select the clock for your region

2. adjust time if necessary

3. select alarm settings

4. set stop watch

5. set timer

Photo Booth

The Photo Booth icon allows you to add different looks to your photos. Some of the options are:

1. Thermal camera

2. Mirror

3. X-Ray

4. Kaleidoscope

5. Normal

6. Light Tunnel

7. Squeeze

8. Twirl

9. Stretch

After making a choice, you can go back to additional options by touching the option on the bottom left and go back to all Apps by pressing the Home button.

Calendar

The Calendar icon has several options, you can have more than one calendar setup in Google Calendar. When you click on the Calendar icon, you are able to:

1. Click on the calendar link

2. The second button allows you to invite others to share/view your calendar

3. You can view the Calendar by day, week, month, year or list view

4. You can also search for information on your Calendar

Notes

When you have things to remember, you can create notes by simply tapping the Notes icon. Notes are added by pressing the + sign. A list of all notes can be found under the Notes tab. At the bottom you can:

1. Go back

2. Write more

3. Delete, or

4. Go forward

Reminders

The Reminders App allows you to select or press the icon, then type any reminders that you may have. Select the day/date on the calendar at the bottom of the App. To go back to the main menu option or the **Home** display, press the **Home** button at the bottom.

Safari

Use **Safari** to get on the Internet, surf the web, and download items and Apps that you would like. Be careful with credit card information and responding to links that you are not familiar with.

Video

Video allows you to download video from the Internet through iTunes.

Music

Music allows you to download music from the Internet and iTunes.

Newsstand

Newsstand allows you to download books, magazines, and etc.

Summary

This resource manual outlines in detail the Apps/features that you are most likely to utilize as you work with your iPad. Reinforcement activities have been added to give you support and practice as you are exposed to concepts and terms.

Sometimes we forget how to operate our iPad, and when we do, all we have to do is go back to this manual. Remember your iPad needs to be setup before attempting to use it.

As you know, you need a phone carrier (AT&T, Verizon, or T-Mobile, etc.) Basic terminology that you will need has been defined. Understanding these terms will help you relate to the procedures and processes that are necessary.

The most important advice that I can give you at this time is, **Do Not Panic**, practice daily and when something does not work the first time, Go back **Home** and try it again. The **Home** button is your friend. When all else fails, turn the iPad off and start again. Thank you for purchasing this manual and let me know if I can help you.

The features associated with using the iPad and the iPhone have been summarized. The icons are basically the same in both. We have reviewed:

*a basic vocabulary--the vocabulary is very important as you try to understand the iPad;

*ways to get started--become familiar with all of the parts of the iPad;

*how to enter text--you can enter text by typing or dictating through **Siri**;

*how to create contacts--messages, and photos, and how to send and receive email; and

*how to have fun with your iPad--the important thing is to take your time and you will have fun learning to use your new technology!

When you do something and it doesn't work the first time, just follow the steps again, and for some reason it works after that (smile). ***Happy iPadding!***

About the Author

Dr. Iburia Hall-Haynes, has been an educator and trainer for more than 40 years. She is co-founder and senior partner of her education and training consulting firm, EBH &T Associates where she provides web development, instructional design, and technology training services to clients.

Dr. Hall-Haynes is a graduate of Alabama State University (B.S., 1972); Antioch University (M.A., 1977); and George Mason University (Ph.D., 2007). She was a teacher, Technology Integration Education Specialist, and Performance Evaluation Program Specialist in the Alexandria City Public Schools in Alexandria, VA for about three decades before retirement. Many of the students, teachers, administrators, and other staff she taught and trained referred to her as a "teacher's teacher" and a "trainer's trainer".

She is an active member of Oakland Baptist Church in Alexandria, VA and Alpha Kappa Alpha Sorority, Inc., as well as a board member of Project Discovery Alexandria. She enjoys giving back to the community and working with Vacation Bible School and dropout and truancy intervention projects.

Writing this manual is an outgrowth of Dr. Hall-Haynes' desire to assist senior citizens and to help her mother learn how to use the iPad and iPhone. *Her mother always finds a way to inspire her.* Designing and developing this manual has been a pure joy for her as she drew on her many years of experience in technology to make it simple, seamless, and fun.

CPSIA information can be obtained
at www.ICGtesting.com
Printed in the USA
LVIC04n1451240815
451319LV00005B/99